Place Your
Photograph
Here

Presented To:

_____

From:

_____

Date:

_____

God's Promises® for American Heroes

Assurance and Hope for
Those Who Serve
and Those Who Wait

Table of Contents ——

Selected Bible Readings

Introduction ———

Because you've opened this book, the chances are high that you are *either* serving America *or* waiting prayerfully for the return of a loved one. In either case, you have earned our nation's heartfelt gratitude. We live in a perilous world, and the forces that seek to destroy our way of life are as determined as they are fanatical. Without heroes like you and yours, we would forfeit the precious freedoms that make America great.

If you're currently serving our nation—either at home or abroad—*or* if you love someone who is, you can find comfort in the promises of God's Holy Word. God offers you assurance and hope *if* you trust Him. When you are fearful, He offers courage; if you are weary, He can renew your soul; when you have questions or doubts, He can reassure you through the promises of His Word. And make no mistake: whether you are stationed halfway around the globe or waiting right here at home, God honors your service.

The teachings of Christ are unambiguous. Those who seek a place of glory in His kingdom must be servants here on earth (Mark 9:35). So, if you—or a loved one— has been called to a position of service to our country, please accept the enduring thanks of a grateful nation. From Maine to California and from the Florida Keys to the Bering Strait, Americans appreciate your sacrifices…and so does God.

This collection of devotional readings contains Bible verses, stories, prayers, and places to record your own personal thoughts. May these pages give you comfort, courage, and strength; and may God bless you *and* your loved ones now and forever.

Adversity

Come to Me, all you who labor and are heavy laden,
and I will give you rest. Take My yoke upon you
and learn from Me for I am gentle and lowly in heart,
and you will find rest for your souls
For My yoke is easy and My burden is light.

Matthew 11:28-30 NKJV

If you're serving our nation at home or abroad—or if your loved one is stationed in a distant land—then you are certainly no stranger to adversity. Thankfully, God's promises offer you assurance and hope.

When we face the inevitable difficulties of life-here-on-earth, God stands ready to protect us. Our responsibility, of course, is to ask Him for protection. When we call upon Him in heartfelt prayer, He will answer—in His own time and in accordance with His own perfect plan.

Are these the toughest of times for you? If so, you must trust in God's power, His mercy, and His grace. For it is only when we place our lives in God's hands that we are truly secure.

*It is true that we endure trials,
but it is also true that we are delivered out of them.*
C. H. *Spurgeon*

A Prayer

Dear Lord, You are indeed my Shepherd.
When I am afraid, You protect me. When I
am discouraged, You lift me up. When I am
lost, You lead me home. Let me turn to You,
Father, for the needs of this day. And
whatever my circumstances, let me trust You
today, tomorrow, and forever.
—*Amen*

My Personal Reflections:_____
_____
_____
_____
_____

Date:_____

Anxiety

In the multitude of my anxieties within me,
Your comforts delight my soul.

Psalm 94:19 NKJV

Because we live in a difficult world, we have understandable fears for our families and our nation. When anxiety fills our hearts, we can turn to God for comfort and assurance. Thankfully, when we earnestly seek Him, God makes His presence known.

Are you worried? Take your worries to God. Are you troubled? Take your troubles to Him. Does the world seem to be trembling beneath your feet? Seek protection from the One who cannot be moved. The same God who created the universe will protect you if you ask Him . . . so ask Him.

*The beginning of anxiety is the end of faith, and the
beginning of true faith is the end of anxiety.*
George Mueller

A Prayer

Lord, sometimes this world is a difficult place,
and, as a frail human being, I am fearful.
When I am worried, restore my faith.
When I am anxious, turn my thoughts to You.
When I grieve, touch my heart with Your
love. And, keep me mindful, Lord, that
nothing, absolutely nothing, will happen this
day that You and I cannot handle together.
—*Amen*

My Personal Reflections:_____

_____

_____

_____

_____

Date:_____

Asking God

So I say to you, ask, and it will be given to you;
seek, and you will find; knock, and it will be opened
to you. For everyone who asks receives,
and he who seeks finds,
and to him who knocks it will be opened.

Luke 11:9-10 NKJV

Sometimes, amid the demands and the frustrations of life-here-on-earth, we forget to slow ourselves down long enough to talk with God. Instead of turning our thoughts and prayers to Him, we rely instead upon our own resources. Instead of praying for strength and courage, we seek to manufacture it within ourselves. Instead of asking God for guidance, we depend only upon our own limited wisdom.

In these difficult days, we need the love, the guidance, and the salvation that can and should be ours when we seek God's wisdom and trust His promises. So if you are worried, fearful, or uncertain about the future, bow your head and have a quiet conversation with the Giver of all good things. When you sincerely lift your heart to God in prayer, He will give you comfort, assurance, wisdom, and hope.

*When you ask God to do something, don't ask timidly;
put your whole heart into it.*

Marie T. Freeman

A Prayer

Lord, when I have questions or fears,
let me turn to You. When I am weak, let me
seek Your strength. When I am discouraged,
Father, keep me mindful of Your love and
Your grace. In all things, let me seek Your will
and Your way, Dear Lord, today and forever.

—*Amen*

My Personal Reflections:_____

_____

_____

_____

Date:_____

Behavior

*Therefore, since we have this ministry, as we have
received mercy, we do not lose heart. But we have
renounced the hidden things of shame, not walking in
craftiness nor handling the word of God deceitfully, but
by manifestation of the truth commending ourselves
to every man's conscience in the sight of God.*

2 Corinthians 4:1-2 NKJV

Life is a series of decisions and choices. Each day, we make countless decisions that can bring us closer to God...or not. When we live according to God's commandments, we earn for ourselves the abundance and peace that He intends for our lives. But, when we turn our backs upon God by disobeying Him, we bring needless suffering upon ourselves and our families.

Do you seek spiritual abundance that can be yours through the person of God's only begotten Son? Then invite Christ into your heart and live according to His teachings. And, when you confront a difficult decision or a powerful temptation, seek God's wisdom and trust it. When you do, you will receive untold blessings—not only for this day, but also for all eternity.

*Resolved: never to do anything which I should be afraid
to do if it were the last hour of my life.*
Jonathan Edwards

A Prayer

Lord, I pray that my actions will always
be consistent with my beliefs. I know that
my deeds speak more loudly than my words.
May every step that I take reflect Your truth
and love, and may others be drawn
to You because of my words and my deeds.
—*Amen*

My Personal Reflections:_____

_____

_____

_____

Date:_____

Blessings

The LORD bless thee, and keep thee:
The LORD make his face shine upon thee,
and be gracious unto thee.

Numbers 6:24-25 KJV

To those whom much is given, much is expected, and so it is with America. Our nation's challenges are great, and no single individual, no matter how wise, can chart the proper course for our nation. But, we the people—under God and respectful of His commandments—can join together to protect and preserve our nation and, in doing so, give protection and hope to freedom-loving people around the globe.

If you sat down and began counting your blessings, how long would it take? A very, very long time! Your blessings include life, freedom, family, friends, talents, and possessions, for starters. But, your greatest blessing—a gift that is yours for the asking—is God's gift of salvation through Christ Jesus. Today, give thanks for your blessings and show your thanks by using them and by sharing them.

Do we not continually pass by blessings innumerable
without notice, and instead fix our eyes on what we feel to
be our trials and our losses, and think and talk about these
until our whole horizon is filled with them, and we almost
begin to think we have no blessings at all?
Hannah Whitall Smith

A Prayer

Lord, You have given me so much,
and I am thankful. Today, I seek
Your continued blessings for my life,
for my family, and for my nation.
Let me share Your gifts with others, and let
my nation show generosity to people
throughout the world. We are blessed that we
might bless others. Let us give thanks for
Your gifts . . . and let us share them.
—*Amen*

My Personal Reflections:_____

_____

_____

_____

Date:_____

Confidence

For You are my hope, O Lord God;
You are my trust from my youth.

Psalm 71:5 NKJV

We Christians have many reasons to be confident. God is in His heaven; Christ has risen, and we are the sheep of His flock. Yet sometimes, even the most devout Christians can become discouraged. Discouragement, however, is not God's way; He is a God of possibility not negativity.

Are you a confident Christian? You should be. God's grace is eternal and His promises are everlasting. So count your blessings, not your hardships. And live courageously. God is the Giver of all things good, and He watches over you today and forever.

*Feelings of confidence depend upon the type of thoughts
you habitually occupy.
Think defeat, and you are bound to be defeated.*
                                            Norman Vincent Peale

A Prayer

Lord, let me turn to You for confidence and
for strength. When I am fearful, keep me
mindful of Your promises. When I am
anxious, let me turn my thoughts and prayers
to the priceless gift of Your Son. You are with
me always, Heavenly Father, and I will face
the challenges of this day with trust
and assurance in You.
—*Amen*

My Personal Reflections:_____
_____
_____
_____
_____
Date:_____

Courage

Be strong and of good courage, and do it; do not fear nor be dismayed, for the LORD God—my God—will be with you. He will not leave you nor forsake you.

1 Chronicles 28:20 NKJV

A storm rose quickly on the Sea of Galilee, and the disciples were afraid. Although they had seen Jesus perform many miracles, the disciples feared for their lives; so they turned to their Savior and He calmed the waters and the wind.

Sometimes, we, like the disciples, feel threatened by the inevitable storms of life. And when we are fearful, we, too, can turn to Christ for courage and for comfort.

The next time your courage is tested to the limit, remember that the One who calmed the wind and the waves is also your personal Savior. And remember that the ultimate battle has already been won at Calvary. We, as believers, can live courageously in the promises of our Lord . . . and we should.

Why rely on yourself and fall? Cast yourself upon His arm. Be not afraid. He will not let you slip. Cast yourself in confidence. He will receive you and heal you.
St. Augustine

A Prayer

Lord, sometimes, this world can be a fearful place, but You have promised me that You are with me always. Today, Lord, I will live courageously as I place my trust in Your everlasting power and my faith in Your everlasting love.
—*Amen*

My Personal Reflections:_____

_____

_____

_____

_____

Date:_____

Death

And God will wipe away every tear from their eyes;
there shall be no more death, nor sorrow, nor crying.
There shall be no more pain, for the former things
have passed away.

Revelation 21:4 NKJV

For Christian believers, death is not an ending; it is a beginning. For Christian believers, the grave is not a final resting place; it is a place of transition. Yet even when we know our loved ones are at peace with Christ, we still weep bitter tears, not so much for the departed but instead for ourselves.

God promises that He is "close to the brokenhearted" (Psalm 34:18). In times of intense sadness, we must turn to Him, and we must encourage our friends and family members to do likewise. Death can never claim those who have accepted Christ as their personal Savior. We have received the gift of life abundant and eternal.

Live in Christ; die in Christ;
and the flesh need not fear death.

John Knox

A Prayer

Lord, You have given Your children the
promise of eternal life through
Your Son Jesus. Keep the hope of heaven fresh
in my heart. And, while I am in this world,
help me to pass through it with faith
in my heart and praise on my lips for You.
—Amen

My Personal Reflections:_____

_____

_____

_____

_____

Date:_____

Difficult Days

When you pass through the waters, I will be with you;
And through the rivers, they shall not overflow you.
When you walk through the fire, you shall not be burned,
Nor shall the flame scorch you.
For I am the LORD your God . . . .

Isaiah 43:2-3 NKJV

Throughout the seasons of life, we must all endure life-altering personal losses that leave us breathless. When we do, God stands ready to protect us. Psalm 147 promises, "He heals the brokenhearted and binds up their wounds" (v. 3 NKJV). And God keeps His promises.

Life is often challenging, but as Christians, we must trust the promises of our Heavenly Father. God loves us, and He will protect us. In times of hardship, He will comfort us; in times of sorrow, He will dry our tears. When we are troubled or weak or sorrowful, God is with us. And His love endures, not only for today but also for all of eternity.

*When the train goes through a tunnel and the world
becomes dark, do you jump out? Of course not.
You sit still and trust the engineer to get you through.*
Corrie ten Boom

A Prayer

Dear Lord, when the day is difficult, give me
perspective and faith. When I am weak, give
me strength. Let me trust in Your promises,
Father, and let me live with the assurance
that You are with me not only today,
but also throughout all eternity.
—*Amen*

My Personal Reflections:_____

_____

_____

_____

_____

Date:_____

Discipline

Buy the truth, and do not sell it,
Also wisdom and instruction and understanding.

Proverbs 23:23 NKJV

The Bible makes it clear: God doesn't reward laziness or misbehavior. To the contrary, God expects His believers to lead lives that are above reproach. And, He punishes those who disobey His commandments.

When we work diligently and live courageously, we can expect a bountiful harvest. But we must never expect the harvest to precede the labor. First, we must lead lives of discipline and obedience; then, we will reap the never-ending rewards that God has promised.

True willpower and courage are not only on the battlefield,
but also in everyday conquests over
our inertia, laziness, and boredom.

D. L. Moody

A Prayer

Heavenly Father, make me a person of
discipline and righteousness.
Let me teach others by the faithfulness of
my conduct, and let me follow Your will
and Your Word, today and every day.

—*Amen*

My Personal Reflections:_____

_____

_____

_____

_____

Date:_____

Doubts

*When doubts filled my mind, your comfort gave me
renewed hope and cheer.*

Psalm 94:19 NKJV

Even the most faithful Christians are overcome by occasional bouts of fear and doubt. You are no different. When you feel that your faith is being tested to its limits, seek the comfort and assurance of the One who sent His Son as a sacrifice for you.

Have you recently felt your faith in God slipping away? If so, you are not alone. Every life—including yours—is a series of successes and failures, celebrations and disappointments, joys and sorrows. But even when we feel very distant from God, God is never distant from us. When we sincerely seek His presence, He will touch our hearts and restore our souls.

There is a difference between doubt and unbelief.
Doubt is a matter of mind: we cannot understand what
God is doing or why He is doing it.
Unbelief is a matter of will: we refuse to believe
God's Word and obey what He tells us to do.
Warren Wiersbe

A Prayer

Dear Lord, when I am filled with uncertainty
and doubt, give me faith. In the dark
moments of life, remind me of Your
faithfulness. Keep me mindful of Your healing
power and Your infinite love, so that
I may live courageously and faithfully
today and every day.
—Amen

My Personal Reflections:_____

_____

_____

_____

_____

Date:_____

Encouraging Others—

A word fitly spoken is like apples of gold in settings of silver.
Proverbs 25:11 NKJV

Plants of every sort respond to nourishment, and so it is with human hearts. When we offer encouragement to our family members, to our friends, or to our fellow servicemen and women, we share a form of nourishment that is vital to our souls.

Today, seek to encourage all who cross your path. Measure your words carefully. Speak wisely, not impulsively. Look for the good that you find in others, and celebrate the good that you find. When you do, you'll be a powerful force of encouragement in the world . . . and a worthy servant to your God.

Encouragement is multiplication:
for every word of encouragement that you share with
someone else, you will likely receive two in return.
Paul Shepherd

A Prayer

Lord, make me mindful of my words.
This world can be a difficult place, and many
of Your children are discouraged and afraid.
Make me a powerful source of encouragement
to those in need, and let my words and deeds
be worthy of Your Son, the One who
gives me courage and strength,
this day and for all eternity.
—*Amen*

My Personal Reflections:_____

_____

_____

_____

Date:_____

Energy

I can do all things through Christ who strengthens me.

Philippians 4:13 NKJV

All of us have moments when we feel drained. All of us suffer through difficult days, trying times, and perplexing periods of our lives. Thankfully, God stands ready and willing to give us comfort and strength if we turn to Him.

If you're a person with too many demands and too few hours in which to meet them, don't fret. Instead, focus upon God and upon His love for you. Then, ask Him for the wisdom to prioritize your life and the strength to fulfill your responsibilities. God will give you the energy to do the most important things on today's to-do list if you ask Him. So ask Him.

Where there is much prayer, there will be much of
the Spirit; where there is much of the Spirit,
there will be ever-increasing power.

Andrew Murray

A Prayer

Lord, let me find my strength in You.
When I am weary, give me rest.
When I feel overwhelmed, let me look to You
for wisdom and for renewal. Let Your power
be my power, Lord, and let Your way be my
way, today and forever.

—Amen

My Personal Reflections:_____

_____

_____

_____

_____

Date:_____

Eternal Life

Let not your heart be troubled; you believe in God,
believe also in Me. In My Father's house are many
mansions; if it were not so, I would have told you.
I go to prepare a place for you. And if I go and prepare
a place for you, I will come again and receive you
to Myself; that where I am, there you may be also.

John 14:1-3 NKJV

Christ sacrificed His life on the cross so that we might have eternal life. This gift, freely given from God's only begotten Son, is the priceless possession of everyone who accepts Him as Lord and Savior.

God is waiting patiently for each of us to accept the gift of eternal life. Let us claim Christ's gift today.

And because we know Christ is alive,
we have hope for the present
and hope for life beyond the grave.

Billy Graham

A Prayer

Lord, I am only here on earth for a brief
while. But, You have offered me the priceless
gift of eternal life through Your Son Jesus.
I accept Your gift, Lord, with thanksgiving
and praise. And, during my brief time in this
world, let me share the good news of
my salvation with those who need
Your healing touch.

—*Amen*

My Personal Reflections:_____

_____

_____

_____

Date:_____

Evil

Be sober, be vigilant; because your adversary the devil walks about like a roaring lion, seeking whom he may devour. Resist him, steadfast in the faith . . . .

1 Peter 5:8-9 NKJV

In his letter to Jewish Christians who had been driven out of Jerusalem, Peter offered a stern warning: ". . . your adversary the devil walks about like a roaring lion, seeking whom he may devour" (1 Peter 5:8 NKJV). What was true in New Testament times is equally true in our own. Satan tempts his prey and then seeks to devour them.

As believers, we must beware; as Americans, we must be vigilant. Evil is indeed abroad in the world, and Satan continues to sow the seeds of destruction far and wide. If we seek righteousness in our own lives and in the collective life of our nation, we must earnestly wrap ourselves in the protection of God's Holy Word. When we do, we are secure.

The only thing necessary for the triumph of evil
is for good men to do nothing.

Edmund Burke

A Prayer

Dear Lord, because You have given
Your children free will, the world
is a place where evil threatens our lives and
our souls. Protect us, Father, from the evils
and temptations of this difficult age. Help us
to trust You, Father, and to obey Your Word,
knowing that Your ultimate victory
over evil is both inevitable and complete.

—Amen

My Personal Reflections:_____

_____

_____

_____

_____

Date:_____

Faith

But Jesus turned him about, and when he saw her,
he said, Daughter, be of good comfort;
thy faith hath made thee whole.
And the woman was made whole from that hour.
                                        Matthew 9:22 KJV

Jesus makes the point clearly and forcefully: His believers shall live by faith. When a suffering woman sought healing by merely touching the hem of His cloak, Jesus replied, "thy faith hath made thee whole." The message to Christians of every generation is clear: live by faith today and every day.

If your faith is being tested to the point of breaking, know that Your Savior is near. If you reach out to Him in faith, He will give you peace and heal your broken spirit. Be content to touch even the smallest fragment of the Master's garment, and He will make you whole.

*Let your faith in Christ be in the quiet confidence that
He will, every day and every moment, keep you as
the apple of His eye, keep you in perfect peace and in the
sure experience of all the light and the strength you need.*
Andrew Murray

A Prayer

Lord, when this world becomes a fearful place,
give me faith. In the dark moments, help me
to remember that You are always near and
that You can overcome any challenge.
And, in the joyous moments, keep me
mindful that every gift comes from You.
In every aspect of my life, Lord,
and in every circumstance, give me faith.
—*Amen*

My Personal Reflections:_____
_____
_____
_____
_____
Date:_____

Family ———————

Beloved, if God so loved us,
we also ought to love one another.

1 John 4:11 NKJV

Even when they are separated by distance and time, our loved ones never really leave us. They are always with us in our hearts and in our prayers.

A loving family is a treasure from God; if you are a member of a close knit, supportive family, offer a word of thanks to Him. He has blessed you with one of His most precious earthly possessions. And, remember that every member of your family is always as near as your next warm memory or your next heartfelt prayer.

Your family is God's gift to you, as you are to them.
Desmond Tutu

A Prayer

Dear Lord, I am blessed to be part of the
family of God where I find love and
acceptance. You have also blessed me with
my earthly family. Today I pray for them;
I pray for all the families in America, and for
families throughout our world. Protect us and
guide us, Lord. And, as I reach out to my own
family, may I show them the same love
and care that You have shown to me.
—*Amen*

My Personal Reflections:_____
_____
_____
_____
_____
Date:_____

Fear

Let not your heart be troubled:
ye believe in God, believe also in me.

John 14:1 KJV

Even dedicated followers of Christ may find their courage tested by the inevitable disappointments and tragedies of life. During our most troubling times, God remains steadfast; as believers, we must turn to Him.

The next time you find your courage tested, remember that God is as near as your next breath, and remember that He offers salvation to His children. He is your shield and your strength. Call upon Him in your hour of need and be comforted. Whatever the size of your challenge, God is bigger.

Perhaps I am stronger than I think.
Thomas Merton

A Prayer

Your Word reminds me, Lord, that even when
I walk through the valley of the shadow of
death, I need fear no evil, for You are with
me, and You comfort me. Thank You, Lord,
for a perfect love that casts out fear.
Let me live courageously and
faithfully this day and every day.
—*Amen*

My Personal Reflections:_____

_____

_____

_____

_____

Date:_____

Forgiveness

*And be kind to one another, tenderhearted,
forgiving one another, just as God in Christ forgave you.*
Ephesians 4:32 NKJV

There's no doubt about it: forgiveness is difficult. Being frail, fallible, imperfect human beings, we are quick to anger, quick to blame, slow to forgive, and even slower to forget. Yet as Christians, we are commanded to forgive others, just as we, too, have been forgiven. So even when forgiveness is difficult, we must ask God to help us move beyond the spiritual stumbling blocks of bitterness and hate.

How should you treat those who have done you great harm? The answer, of course, is found in God's Word: you are instructed to forgive them. When you do, you will not only obey God's commandment; you will also free yourself from a prison of your own making.

*He who cannot forgive others breaks
the bridge over which he himself must pass.*
                                        Corrie ten Boom

A Prayer
Heavenly Father, forgiveness is
Your commandment, and I know that
I should forgive others just as You have
forgiven me. But, genuine forgiveness is
difficult. Help me to forgive those who have
injured me, and deliver me from the traps
of anger and bitterness. Forgiveness
is Your way, Lord; let it be mine.
                —*Amen*

My Personal Reflections:_____
_____
_____
_____
_____
Date:_____

God's Grace

For by grace are ye saved through faith;
and that not of yourselves: it is the gift of God:
not of works, lest any man should boast.

Ephesians 2:8-9 KJV

Christ sacrificed His life on the cross so that we might have life eternal. This gift, freely given from God's only begotten Son, is the priceless possession of everyone who accepts Him as Lord and Savior. Thankfully, grace is not an earthly reward for righteous behavior; it is, instead, a blessed spiritual gift. When we accept Christ into our hearts, we are saved by His grace.

God's grace is the ultimate gift, and we owe to Him the ultimate in thanksgiving. Let us praise the Creator for His priceless gift, and let us share the Good News with the world. We return our Father's love by accepting His grace and by sharing His message and His love. When we do, we are eternally blessed. God is waiting patiently for each of us to accept His gift of eternal life. Let us claim Christ's gift today.

All men who live with any degree of serenity live
by some assurance of grace.

Reinhold Niebuhr

A Prayer

Dear Lord, You have given Your grace freely
through Christ Jesus. I praise You for that
priceless gift. Let me share the Good News of
Your Son with a world that desperately needs
His peace, His abundance, His love,
and His salvation.

—*Amen*

My Personal Reflections:_____

_____

_____

_____

Date:_____

God's Love

For God so loved the world that He gave His only begotten Son, that whoever believes in Him should not perish but have everlasting life.

John 3:16 NKJV

God's love for you is deeper and more profound than you can fathom. And now, precisely because you are a wondrous creation treasured by God, a question presents itself: What will you do in response to God's love? Will you ignore it or embrace it? Will you return it or neglect it? The decision, of course, is yours and yours alone.

When you embrace God's love, you are forever changed. When you embrace God's love, you feel differently about yourself, your neighbors, and your world. When you embrace God's love, you share His message and you obey His commandments. When you accept the Father's grace and share His love, you are blessed here on earth and throughout all eternity. Accept His love today.

*The great love of God is an ocean
without a bottom or a shore.*

C. H. *Spurgeon*

A Prayer

Thank You, Dear God, for Your love. You are
my loving Father. I thank You for Your love
and for Your Son. I will praise You,
I will worship You, I will obey You, and I will
love You today, tomorrow, and forever.

—*Amen*

My Personal Reflections:_____

_____

_____

_____

Date:_____

God's Plan

For now we see in a mirror, dimly, but then face to face.
Now I know in part, but then I shall know
just as I also am known.

1 Corinthians 13:12 NKJV

God has plans for our lives and for our nation, but He won't force us to follow His will. To the contrary, He has given us free will, both as individuals and as a people. And, of course, with the freedom to choose comes the responsibility of living with the consequences of the choices we make.

Let us, as standard-bearers of the American Dream, seek guidance through the study of God's Word, and let us be watchful for His signs. God has richly blessed our nation, and He intends to use America in wonderful, unexpected ways. May we discover God's plan for our land, and may we follow it.

*God brought me here. It is by His will that I am in
this place. He will keep me here in His love and give me
grace to behave as His child. He will make this trial
a blessing, teaching me the lessons He intends for me to
learn and working in me the grace He means to bestow.
Then, in His good time He can bring me out again.
How and when, only He knows.*

Andrew Murray

A Prayer

Dear Lord, give me the wisdom to follow
Your direction for my life's journey. Let me do
Your work here on earth by seeking Your will
and living it, knowing that when I trust in
You, Father, I am eternally blessed.

—*Amen*

My Personal Reflections:_____

_____

_____

_____

_____

Date:_____

God's Presence————

Be still, and know that I am God . . . .

Psalm 46:10 KJV

If God is everywhere, why does He sometimes seem so far away? The answer to that question, of course, has nothing to do with God and everything to do with us.

As our burdens weigh down upon us, we are tempted to ignore God's presence or—worse yet—to rebel against His commandments. But, when we quiet ourselves and acknowledge His presence, He touches our hearts and restores our spirits.

In whatever condition we find ourselves, whether we are happy or sad, victorious or vanquished, troubled or triumphant, we must seek the quiet assurance of our Heavenly Father. When we do so, we will be comforted, for God is not just near—He is here.

*God is in all things and in every place. There is not
a place in the world in which he is not most truly present.
Just as birds, wherever they fly, always meet with the air,
so we, wherever we go, or wherever we are,
always find God present.*

St. Francis de Sales

A Prayer

Dear Lord, You are always with me and
You are always listening
to my thoughts and to my prayers.
Let me pray to You often,
and let me trust in You always.
—*Amen*

My Personal Reflections:_____

_____

_____

_____

_____

Date:_____

God's Promises———

For you have need of endurance,
so that after you have done the will of God,
you may receive the promise.

Hebrews 10:36 NKJV

God's Word contains promises upon which we, as Christians, can and must depend. The Bible is a priceless gift, a tool that God intends for us to use in every aspect of our lives. Too many Christians, however, keep their spiritual tool kits tightly closed and out of sight.

Are you tired? Discouraged? Fearful? Be comforted and trust the promises that God has made to you. Do you see a difficult future ahead? Be courageous and call upon God. He will protect you and then use you according to His purposes. Are you confused? Listen to the quiet voice of your Heavenly Father. He is not a God of confusion. Talk with Him; listen to Him; trust Him, and trust His promises. He is steadfast, and He is your Protector . . . forever.

No one who has ever set out to test God's promises fairly, thoroughly, and humbly has ever had to report that God's promises don't work. On the contrary, given a fair opportunity, God always surprises and overwhelms those who truly seek His bounty and His power.

Peter Marshall

A Prayer
Lord, Your Holy Word contains promises, and I will trust them. I will use the Bible as my guide, and I will trust You, Lord, to speak to me through Your Holy Spirit and through Your Holy Word, this day and forever.

—*Amen*

My Personal Reflections:_____

_____

_____

_____

_____

Date:_____

God's Strength

He said unto me, My grace is sufficient for thee:
for my strength is made perfect in weakness.

2 Corinthians 12:9 KJV

Have you "tapped in" to the power of God? Have you turned your life and your heart over to Him, or are you muddling along under your own power? The answer to this question will determine the quality of your life here on earth and the destiny of your life throughout all eternity.

The Bible tells us that we can do all things through the power of Jesus Christ. Thus we must place Christ where He belongs: at the very center of our lives. When we do so, we will surely discover that He offers us the strength to live victoriously in this world and eternally in the next.

*The last and greatest lesson that the soul has to learn is
the fact that God, and God alone, is enough for all
its needs. This is the lesson that all His dealings with us
are meant to teach; and this is the crowning discovery of
our whole Christian life. God is enough!*
Hannah Whitall Smith

A Prayer

Lord, You have promised never to leave me
or forsake me. You are always with me,
protecting me and encouraging me. Whatever
this day may bring, I thank You for Your love
and for Your strength. Let me lean upon You,
Father, this day and forever.
—*Amen*

My Personal Reflections:_____
_____
_____
_____
_____
Date:_____

God's Support ————

For I the LORD thy God will hold thy right hand,
saying unto thee, Fear not; I will help thee.

Isaiah 41:13 KJV

God is a never-ending source of support and courage for those of us who call upon Him. When we are weary, He gives us strength. When we see no hope, God reminds us of His promises. When we grieve, God wipes away our tears.

Do the demands of this day threaten to overwhelm you? If so, you must rely not only upon your own resources, but also upon the promises of your Father in heaven. God will hold your hand and walk with you every day of your life if you let Him. So even if your circumstances are difficult, trust the Father. His love is eternal and His goodness endures forever.

When you have no helpers, see all your helpers in God.
When you have many helpers, see God in all your helpers.
When you have nothing but God, see all in God;
when you have everything, see God in everything.
Under all conditions, stay thy heart only on the Lord.
                                                C. H. Spurgeon

A Prayer
Dear Lord, You have promised that You will
provide for my needs, and I trust that promise.
But sometimes, because of my imperfect faith,
I fall prey to worry and doubt. Today,
give me the courage to trust You completely.
You are my protector, Father. Let me
love You, and let me trust in
the perfect wisdom of Your plan.
—*Amen*

My Personal Reflections:_____
_____
_____
_____
_____
Date:_____

God's Will

Trust in the LORD with all thine heart;
and lean not unto thine own understanding.
In all thy ways acknowledge him,
and he shall direct thy paths.

Proverbs 3:5-6 KJV

As human beings with limited understanding, we can never fully understand the will of God. But as believers in a benevolent Father, we must always trust the will of God.

When Jesus went to the Mount of Olives, as described in Luke 22, He poured out His heart to God. Jesus knew of the agony that He was destined to endure, but He also knew that God's will must be done. We, like our Savior, face trials that bring fear and trembling to the very depths of our souls, but like Christ, we too must ultimately seek God's will, not our own.

Faith is the belief that God will do what is right.
                                        Max Lucado

A Prayer

Dear Lord, You have a plan for me and a plan
for this world. Let me trust Your will, and let
me discover Your plan for my life so that I can
become the person You want me to become.
                    —Amen

My Personal Reflections:_____

_____

_____

_____

Date:_____

Grief

Blessed are those who mourn, for they shall be comforted.
Matthew 5:4 NKJV

Grief visits all of us who live long and love deeply. When we lose a loved one, or when we experience any other profound loss, darkness overwhelms us for awhile, and it seems as if we cannot summon the strength to face another day—but, with God's help, we can.

When our friends or family members encounter life-shattering events, we struggle to find words that might offer them comfort and support. But finding the right words can be difficult, if not impossible. Thankfully, God promises that He is "near to those who have a broken heart" (Psalm 34:18 NKJV). In times of intense sadness, we must turn to Him, and we must encourage our friends and family members to do likewise. When we do, our Father comforts us and, in time, He heals us.

*Tears are permitted to us,
but they must glisten in the light of faith and hope.*
C. H. Spurgeon

A Prayer

Lord, You have promised that You will not give us more than we can bear; You have promised to lift us out of our grief and despair; You have promised to put a new song on our lips. Today, Lord, I pray for those who mourn, and I thank You for sustaining all of us in our days of sorrow. May we trust You always and praise You forever.

—*Amen*

My Personal Reflections:_____

_____

_____

_____

_____

Date:_____

Guilt

For all have sinned, and come short of the glory of God.
Romans 3:23 KJV

All of us have sinned. Sometimes our sins result from our own stubborn rebellion against God's commandments. And sometimes, we are swept up in events that are beyond our abilities to control. Under either set of circumstances, we may experience intense feelings of guilt. But God has an answer for the guilt that we feel. That answer, of course, is His forgiveness. When we confess our wrongdoings and repent from them, we are forgiven by the One who created us.

Are you troubled by feelings of guilt or regret? If so, you must repent from your misdeeds, and you must ask your Heavenly Father for His forgiveness. When you do so, He will forgive you completely and without reservation. Then, you must forgive yourself just as God has forgiven you: thoroughly and unconditionally.

Don't be bound by your guilt or your fears any longer,
but realize that sin's penalty has already been paid
by Christ completely and fully.

Billy Graham

A Prayer
Dear Lord, I am an imperfect human being.
When I have sinned, let me repent from my
wrongdoings, and let me seek forgiveness—
first from You, then from others,
and finally from myself.
—*Amen*

My Personal Reflections:_____

_____

_____

_____

_____

Date:_____

Healing

The Lord is my shepherd; I shall not want.
He makes me to lie down in green pastures;
He leads me beside the still waters. He restores my soul.
Psalm 23:1-3 NKJV

God's Word has much to say about every aspect of your life, including your health. And, when you encounter concerns of any sort—including health-related challenges—you must remember that God is with you and that He will never desert you.

If you are suffering—either physically, emotionally, or spiritually—you should call upon every resource that is available to you, starting with God. So trust your medical doctors to do their part, but place your ultimate trust in a benevolent Heavenly Father. His healing touch, like His love, endures forever.

He is the God of wholeness and restoration.
Stormie Omartian

A Prayer

Dear Lord, place Your healing hand upon me.
Heal my body and my soul. Let me trust
Your promises, Father, and let me turn to You
for hope, for restoration, for renewal,
and for salvation.
—*Amen*

My Personal Reflections:_____
_____
_____
_____
_____

Date:_____

Honor

*Blessed are those who hunger and thirst for righteousness,
for they shall be filled.*

Matthew 5:6 NKJV

As the familiar saying goes, "Honesty is the best policy." But for believers, it is far more important to note that honesty is God's policy. And if we are to be servants worthy of our Savior, Jesus Christ, we must be honest and forthright in all our dealings with others. Sometimes, of course, doing the honorable thing is difficult. Sometimes, honesty is painful. But honesty is always God's way.

Sometime soon, perhaps even today, you will be tempted to bend the truth or perhaps even to break it. Resist that temptation. Truth is God's way, and it must also be your way, too.

Peace, if possible, but truth at any rate.

Martin Luther

A Prayer

Dear Lord, You command Your children to behave honorably. Let me follow Your commandment. Give me the courage to speak honestly and to walk righteously with You so that others might see Your eternal truth reflected in my words and my deeds.

—*Amen*

My Personal Reflections:_____

_____

_____

_____

Date:_____

Hope

But I will hope continually,
And will praise You yet more and more.

Psalm 71:14 NKJV

Despite God's promises, despite Christ's love, and despite our countless blessings, we frail human beings can still lose hope from time to time. When we do, we need the encouragement of Christian friends, the life-changing power of prayer, and the healing truth of God's Holy Word.

If we find ourselves falling into the spiritual traps of worry and discouragement, we should seek the healing touch of Jesus and the encouraging words of fellow Christians. Even though this world can be a place of trials and struggles, God has promised us peace, joy, and eternal life if we give ourselves to Him. And, of course, God keeps His promises today, tomorrow, and forever.

*Never yield to gloomy anticipation. Place your hope
and confidence in God. He has no record of failure.*
                                Mrs. Charles E. Cowman

A Prayer
Dear Lord, You are my sovereign God.
Your Son defeated death; He overcame
the world; He gives me life abundant
and eternal. Your Holy Spirit comforts
and guides me. Let me celebrate all Your gifts,
and make me a hope-filled Christian today
and every day that I live.
—*Amen*

My Personal Reflections:_____
_____
_____
_____
_____
Date:_____

Inner Strength

Therefore whoever hears these sayings of Mine,
and does them, I will liken him to a wise man
who built his house on the rock.

Matthew 7:24 NKJV

The Bible contains promises, made by God, upon which we can and must depend. But sometimes, especially when we find ourselves caught in the inevitable entanglements of life, we fail to trust God completely.

If you are tired, discouraged, worried, or fearful. Find comfort in God's power and trust the promises that He has made to you. If the road ahead becomes rough or if you get lost; call on God. He will find you and protect you and use you according to His purposes. Pray to Him; hear Him; love Him; trust Him, and trust His promises.

Do not lose faith in God. The grace He gives will be in direct proportion to the amount of sufferings you must bear. No one else can do this except the Creator who made us and knows how to renew our strength by His grace.

Fénelon

A Prayer

Dear Lord, let me turn to You for strength. When I am weak, You lift me up. When my spirit is crushed, You comfort me. When I am victorious, Your Word reminds me to be humble. Today and every day, I will turn to You, Father, for strength, for hope, for wisdom, and for salvation.

—*Amen*

My Personal Reflections:_____

_____

_____

_____

_____

Date:_____

Jesus

Jesus Christ is the same yesterday, today, and forever.
Hebrews 13:8 NKJV

Our circumstances change but Jesus does not. Even when the world seems to be trembling between our feet, Jesus remains the spiritual bedrock that cannot be moved.

The old familiar hymn begins, "What a friend we have in Jesus . . . ." No truer words were ever penned. Jesus is the sovereign Friend and ultimate Savior of mankind. Christ showed enduring love for His believers by willingly sacrificing His own life so that we might have eternal life. Let us love Him, praise Him, and share His message of salvation with our neighbors and with the world.

The crucial question for each of us is this:
What do you think of Jesus,
and do you yet have a personal acquaintance with Him?
Hannah Whitall Smith

A Prayer

Thank You, Lord, for Your Son Jesus.
You loved this world so dearly, Father, that
You sent Your Son to die so that we,
Your children, might have life eternal.
I am grateful for that priceless gift.
Let the love of Jesus be reflected in my words,
my thoughts, and my deeds. And, let me
share His transforming message with
a world in desperate need of His peace.
—*Amen*

My Personal Reflections:_____

_____

_____

_____

Date:_____

Kindness————————

Bear one another's burdens,
and so fulfill the law of Christ.

Galatians 6:2 NKJV

Kindness is God's commandment. Matthew 25:40 warns, " . . . Verily I say unto you, Inasmuch as ye have done it unto one of the least of these my brethren, ye have done it unto me" (KJV). When we extend the hand of friendship to those who need it most, God promises His blessings. When we ignore the needs of others—or mistreat them—we risk God's retribution.

Today, slow yourself down and be alert for those who need your smile, your kind words, or your helping hand. Make kindness a centerpiece of your dealings with others. They will be blessed, and you will be too. When you spread a heaping helping of encouragement and hope to the world, you can't help getting a little bit on yourself.

If we have the true love of God in our hearts, we will show it in our lives. We will not have to go up and down the earth proclaiming it. We will show it in everything we say or do.
D. L. Moody

A Prayer

Dear Lord, let me treat others as I wish to be
treated. Because I expect kindness,
let me be kind. Because I wish to be loved,
let me be loving. Because I need forgiveness,
let me be merciful. In all things, Lord,
let me live by the Golden Rule, and
let me teach that rule to others through
my words and my deeds.
—Amen

My Personal Reflections:_____

_____

_____

_____

Date:_____

Laughter

A merry heart does good, like medicine,
But a broken spirit dries the bones.

Proverbs 17:22 NKJV

Laughter is medicine for the soul, but sometimes, amid the stresses of the day, we forget to take our medicine. Instead of viewing our world with a mixture of optimism and humor, we allow worries and distractions to rob us of the joy that God intends for our lives.

Even if your circumstances are difficult, you should, to the best of your abilities, approach life with a smile on your lips and hope in your heart. After all, God created laughter for a reason . . . and Father indeed knows best. So laugh!

Mirth is God's medicine. Everybody ought to bathe in it.
Henry Ward Beecher

A Prayer
Dear Lord, laughter is Your gift. Today and
every day, put a smile on my face, and
let me share that smile with those
who cross my path . . .
and let me laugh.
—*Amen*

My Personal Reflections:_____

_____

_____

_____

Date:_____

Leadership

Having then gifts differing according to the grace that is given to us, let us use them: if prophecy, let us prophesy in proportion to our faith; he who leads, with diligence; he who shows mercy, with cheerfulness.

Romans 12:6, 8 NKJV

If you are in a position of leadership—whether in the military *or* as a leader at church, work, home, or school—it's up to you to set the right tone by maintaining a proper attitude *and* by setting a proper example.

Are you the kind of leader whom you would want to follow. If so, congratulations. But if the answer to that question is no, then it's time to improve your leadership skills, beginning with the words that you speak and the example that you set, but not necessarily in that order.

You can never separate a leader's actions from his character.
John Maxwell

A Prayer
Heavenly Father, when I find myself in
a position of leadership, let me follow Your
teachings and obey Your commandments.
Make me a person of integrity and wisdom,
Lord, and make me a worthy example to those
whom I serve. And, let me turn to You, Lord,
for guidance and for strength
in all that I say and do.
—Amen

My Personal Reflections:_____
_____
_____
_____
_____

Date:_____

Life

I have come that they may have life,
and that they may have it more abundantly.

John 10:10 NKJV

Every day that we awaken, we are confronted with countless opportunities to serve God and to worship Him. When we do, He blesses us. But, when we turn our backs to the Creator, or when we are simply too busy to acknowledge His greatness, we do a profound disservice to ourselves, to our families, and to our nation.

Life is a glorious opportunity to place ourselves in the service of the One who is the Giver of all blessings. May we seek His will, trust His Word, and place Him where He belongs: at the center of our lives.

Each stage of life has its special duties; by accomplishing them, one may find happiness.

St. Nicholas of Flue

A Prayer

Lord, You are the Giver of all life,
and You created me to have fellowship with
You. Let me live a life that pleases You,
Lord, and let me thank You always for
Your blessings. You love me and protect me,
Heavenly Father. Let me be grateful,
and let me live for You today
and throughout eternity.

—Amen

My Personal Reflections:_____

_____

_____

_____

_____

Date:_____

Love

And now abide faith, hope, love, these three;
but the greatest of these is love.

1 Corinthians 13:13 NKJV

Perhaps your loved ones are removed from you by distance or time. If so, you must remember that love transcends both time and distance.

The familiar words of 1 Corinthians 13 remind us that love is God's commandment. Faith is important, of course. So, too, is hope. But, love is more important still. Yet sometimes, despite our best intentions, we fail to obey our Lord. When we become embittered with ourselves, with our neighbors, or most especially with God, we disobey the One who gave His life for us. Christ showed His love for us on the cross, and, as Christians, we are called upon to return Christ's love by sharing it. Today, let us spread Christ's love to families, to friends, and to strangers—by our words and by our deeds.

He who is filled with love is filled with God Himself.
St. Augustine

A Prayer

Lord, You have given me the gift of eternal
love; let me share that gift with the world.
Help me, Father, to show kindness to those
who cross my path, and let me show
tenderness and unfailing love to my family
and friends. And, help me always to reflect
the love that Christ gave to me so that
through me, others might find Him.
—*Amen*

My Personal Reflections:_____

_____

_____

_____

_____

Date:_____

Miracles

But Jesus looked at them and said to them,
"With men this is impossible,
but with God all things are possible."

Matthew 19:26 NKJV

Sometimes, because we are imperfect human beings with limited understanding and limited faith, we place limitations on God. But, God's power has no limitations. God will work miracles in our lives if we trust Him with everything we have and everything we are. When we do, we experience the miraculous results of His endless love and His awesome power.

Do you lack the faith that God can work miracles in your own life? If so, it's time to reconsider. Are you a "Doubting Thomas" or a "Negative Ned"? If so, you are attempting to place limitations on a God who has none. Instead, you must trust in God and trust in His power. Then, you must wait patiently . . . because something miraculous is about to happen.

Are you looking for a miracle? If you keep your eyes wide open and trust in God, you won't have to look very far.
Marie T. Freeman

A Prayer

Dear Lord, absolutely nothing is impossible for You. Let me trust in Your power and in Your miracles. When I lose hope, give me faith; when others lose hope, let me tell them of Your glorious works. Today, Lord, keep me mindful that You are a God of infinite possibilities and infinite love.

—*Amen*

My Personal Reflections:_____
_____
_____
_____
_____

Date:_____

Obedience to God——

For this is the love of God,
that we keep His commandments,
And His commandments are not burdensome.

1 John 2:5-6 NKJV

God's laws are eternal and unchanging: obedience leads to abundance and joy; disobedience leads to disaster. God has given us a guidebook for righteous living called the Holy Bible. If we trust God's Word and live by it, we are blessed. But, if we choose to ignore God's commandments, the results are as predictable as they are tragic.

Do you seek God's blessings? Then obey Him. When you're faced with a difficult choice or a powerful temptation, seek God's counsel and trust the counsel He gives. Invite God into your heart and live according to His commandments. When you do, you will be blessed today and forever.

God's mark is on everything that obeys Him.
Martin Luther

A Prayer

Dear Lord, when I am tempted to disobey
Your commandments, correct my errors and
guide my path. Make me a faithful steward of
my talents, my opportunities, and
my possessions so that Your kingdom
may be glorified, now and forever.
—*Amen*

My Personal Reflections:_____

_____

_____

_____

_____

Date:_____

Obedience to Our Leaders

Obey those who rule over you, and be submissive,
for they watch out for your souls,
as those who must give account.

Hebrews 13:17 NKJV

All of us are called upon to submit to various forms of authority. In response, we must choose either to obey the orders that we receive—or not. When we obey the honorable directives of our superiors, our obedience is in accordance with God's Word.

Phillip Brooks advised, "Be such a person, and live such a life, that if every person were such as you, and every life a life like yours, this earth would be God's Paradise." And that's sound advice because our superiors are watching . . . and, for that matter, so is God.

*He who has never learned to obey
cannot be a good commander.*

Aristotle

A Prayer

Dear Lord, make me an obedient servant
to You and to those whom You have placed
in positions of leadership. Let my actions
be consistent with Your will for my life.
Let me honor You with every step that I take,
and let me live a life that clearly
demonstrates the love that I feel for
You and for Your Son Jesus.
—*Amen*

My Personal Reflections:_____

_____

_____

_____

_____

Date:_____

Optimism

*Be of good courage, and he shall strengthen your heart,
all ye that hope in the LORD.*

Psalm 31:24 KJV

When we are separated from our loved ones by great distances, we worry. Yet as Christians we have every reason to be optimistic about life. A. W. Tozer writes, "Attitude is all-important. Let the soul take a quiet attitude of faith and love toward God, and from there on, the responsibility is God's. He will make good on His commitments." These words remind us that even when the challenges of the day seem daunting, and even when our hearts are broken, God remains steadfast. And, so must we.

The next time you find yourself falling prey to the blight of pessimism, stop yourself, turn your thoughts around, and give yourself the gift of optimism. And if you see your glass as "half-empty," open your heart to God. With Him, your glass is never half empty. With God as your Protector and Christ as your Savior, your glass is filled to the brim and overflowing . . . forever.

The essence of optimism is that it takes no account of the present, but it is a source of inspiration, of vitality, and of hope. Where others have resigned, it enables a man to hold his head high, to claim the future for himself, and not abandon it to his enemy.

Dietrich Bonhoeffer

A Prayer

Lord, let me expect the best from You, and let me look for the best in others. If I become discouraged, Father, turn my thoughts and my prayers to You. Let me trust You to direct my life. And, let me be Your faithful, hopeful, optimistic servant every day that I live.

—*Amen*

My Personal Reflections:_____

_____

_____

_____

_____

Date:_____

Patience

But if we hope for what we do not see,
we eagerly wait for it with perseverance.

Romans 8:25 NKJV

Life demands patience . . . and lots of it! We live in an imperfect world inhabited by imperfect people. Sometimes, we inherit troubles from others, and sometimes we create trouble for ourselves. In either case, what's required is patience. Lamentations 3:25-26 reminds us that, "The LORD is good to those who wait for Him, To the soul who seeks Him. It is good that one should hope and wait quietly For the salvation of the LORD" (NKJV). But, for most of us, waiting quietly for God is difficult. Why? Because we are fallible human beings, sometimes quick to anger and sometimes slow to forgive.

Are you impatient for your Heavenly Father to reveal His plans and to bestow His blessings? If so, remember that the world unfolds according to God's timetable, not our own. Sometimes, we must wait patiently, and that's as it should be. After all, think how patient God has been with us.

Patience is the companion of wisdom.

St. Augustine

A Prayer

Heavenly Father, give me patience. Let me
live according to Your plan and according to
Your timetable. When I am hurried, slow me
down. When I become impatient with others,
give me empathy. When I am frustrated by
the demands of the day, give me peace. Today,
let me be a patient Christian, Dear Lord,
as I trust in You and in Your master plan.

—*Amen*

My Personal Reflections:_____

_____

_____

_____

_____

Date:_____

Peace

Peace I leave with you, My peace I give to you;
not as the world gives do I give to you.
Let not your heart be troubled, neither let it be afraid.
John 14:27 NKJV

As a godly nation, we seek peace but not peace at all costs. When our nation is threatened, we must defend it or risk losing the liberties that we hold dear. Yet, even when we struggle against forces that would destroy us, we pray for the ultimate victory: lasting peace.

Today, as a gift to yourself, to your family, to your friends, and to your nation, pray for peace in the world and for peace within your soul. Then, claim the inner peace that is your spiritual birthright: the peace that God intends for your life. It is offered freely; it has been paid for in full; it is yours for the asking. So ask. And then share.

Christ alone can bring lasting peace—peace with God—
peace among men and nations—
and peace within our hearts.

Billy Graham

A Prayer

Dear Lord, I pray for peace in the world and
peace within my soul. You are the Giver of all
things good, Father, and You give me peace
when I draw close to You. Help me to trust
Your will, to follow Your commands, and to
accept Your peace, today and forever.

—*Amen*

My Personal Reflections:_____

_____

_____

_____

_____

Date:_____

Perseverance ———————

And let us not grow weary while doing good,
for in due season we shall reap if we do not lose heart.
                                        Galatians 6:9 NKJV

As Americans living in a difficult and dangerous world, we know that the key to success, both as individuals and as a nation, is often nothing more than a willingness to persevere. Sometimes, however, when the storm clouds form overhead and we find ourselves in the dark valley of despair, our faith is stretched to the breaking point. Yet wherever we find ourselves, whether at the top of the mountain or the depths of the valley, God is there, and because He cares for us, we can live courageously.

The next time you find your courage tested to the limit, remember that God is as near as your next breath, and remember that He offers strength and comfort to His children. Whatever your challenge, whatever your trouble, God can help you persevere. And will.

Keep adding, keep walking, keep advancing;
do not stop, do not turn back,
do not turn from the straight road.

St. Augustine

A Prayer

Lord, when life is difficult, I am tempted
to abandon hope in the future.
But You are my God, and I can draw strength
from You. Let me trust You, Father,
in good times and in bad times. Let me
persevere—even if my soul is troubled—
and let me follow Your Son Jesus Christ
this day and forever.
—*Amen*

My Personal Reflections:_____
_____
_____
_____
_____
Date:_____

Prayer

Rejoice always, pray without ceasing,
in everything give thanks;
for this is the will of God in Christ Jesus for you.
1 Thessalonians 5:16-18 NKJV

Prayer changes things and it changes us. Today, instead of turning things over in your mind, turn them over to God in prayer. Instead of worrying about your next decision, decide to let God lead the way.

When you weave the habit of prayer into the very fabric of your day, you invite God to become a partner in every aspect of your life. So don't limit your prayers to meals or to bedtime. Pray constantly about things great and small. God is listening, and He wants to hear from you. Now.

Only God can move mountains,
but faith and prayer can move God.

E. M. Bounds

A Prayer

Dear Lord, Your Holy Word commands me to pray without ceasing. Let me take everything to You in prayer. When I am discouraged, let me pray. When I am lonely, let me take my sorrows to You. When I grieve, let me take my tears to You, Lord, in prayer. And when I am joyful, let me offer up prayers of thanksgiving. In all things and at all times, let me seek Your wisdom and Your grace . . . in prayer.

—Amen

My Personal Reflections:_____

_____

_____

_____

_____

Date:_____

Renewal

*But those who wait on the LORD shall renew their strength;
They shall mount up with wings like eagles, They shall run
and not be weary, They shall walk and not faint.*

Isaiah 40:31 NKJV

When we genuinely lift our hearts and prayers to God, He renews our strength. Are you almost too weary to lift your head? Then bow it. Offer your concerns and your fears to your Father in heaven. He is always at your side, offering His love and His strength.

Are you weak or worried? Delve deeply into God's Holy Word and sense His presence in quiet moments of meditation and prayer. Are you spiritually exhausted? Call upon fellow believers to support you, and call upon Christ to renew your spirit and your life. Your Savior will never let you down.

God is not running an antique shop!
He is making all things new!

Vance Havner

A Prayer

Lord, You are my rock and my strength.
When I grow weary, let me turn
my thoughts and my prayers to You.
When I am discouraged, restore my faith
in You. Let me always trust in Your promises,
Lord, and let me draw strength from those
promises and from Your unending love.
—Amen

My Personal Reflections:_____

_____

_____

_____

_____

Date:_____

Sacrifice

So let each one give as he purposes in his heart,
not grudgingly or of necessity;
for God loves a cheerful giver.

2 Corinthians 9:7 NKJV

The fight for freedom is not a dress rehearsal; it takes place in a real world with real enemies and real dangers. And the American Dream is alive and well because of the brave men and women who serve and protect us.

As Americans of this generation, we have a grand opportunity: we can leave an enduring legacy to our children. That legacy, of course, is a nation strong and free, and we, as protectors of liberty's flame, must do our utmost to leave to the next generation a better nation than the one we received from the last.

May our own personal sacrifices be worthy of those who sacrificed so much to ensure that the Dream would never die. And may God Bless America forever.

We must be willing, individually and as a nation,
to accept whatever sacrifices may be required of us.
A nation that values its privileges above its principles
soon loses both.

Dwight D. Eisenhower

A Prayer

Dear Lord, when I am called upon to make
sacrifices for causes that are just, give me
courage. Let my words and deeds be pleasing
to You, and let my service to others be worthy
of the One who sacrificed His life for mine.

—Amen

My Personal Reflections:_____

_____

_____

_____

_____

Date:_____

Those Who Serve——

But whoever desires to become great among you,
let him be your servant. And whoever desires to be
first among you, let him be your slave—just as the Son
of Man did not come to be served, but to serve,
and to give His life a ransom for many."

Matthew 20:26-28 NKJV

Amrica owes its undying gratitude to those brave men and women who serve in our armed forces. Without them, the promise of this great nation would remain unfulfilled.

Since its earliest days, America has truly been "one nation, under God." And, the Word of God instructs us that service to others is one way of fulfilling His purpose here on earth. Romans 12:10 reminds us, "Be kindly affectionate to one another with brotherly love" (NKJV). Thankfully, Americans of every generation have heeded these words.

If you have chosen a life of service, please accept the profound thanks of Americans everywhere. And above all, keep up the good work . . . Uncle Sam still needs you, and so do the rest of us.

*We Americans understand freedom; we have earned it,
we have lived for it, and we have died for it. This nation
and its people are freedom's models in a searching world.
We can be freedom's missionaries in a doubting world.*
Barry Goldwater

A Prayer
Dear Lord, make me Your faithful servant.
And as I serve my fellow citizens and my
nation, let me do so with courage, with
compassion, and with undying faith in You.
—*Amen*

My Personal Reflections:_____

_____

_____

_____

Date:_____

Those Who Wait ———

The LORD is good to those who wait for Him,
To the soul who seeks Him. It is good that one should hope
and wait quietly For the salvation of the LORD.

Lamentations 3:25-26 NKJV

If you've chosen a life of military or government service, you know that your family pays a price for the sacrifices you make. If you work extended hours, your family feels your absence. If you travel far from home, your family waits anxiously for your return. If you place your life in danger, your family wonders and worries . . . constantly.

America pays tribute to its heroes, of course, but she also pays tribute to those who keep the home fires burning. A grateful nation celebrates "those who wait" because, as we all know, families also serve.

They also serve who only stand and wait.
John Milton

A Prayer

Dear Lord, I am blessed to be part of
the family of God where I find love and
acceptance. You have also blessed me with
my earthly family. Today I pray for them;
I pray for all the families in America, and for
families throughout our world. Protect us and
guide us, Lord. And, as I reach out to my own
family, may I show them the same love
and care that You have shown to me.
—*Amen*

My Personal Reflections:_____

_____

_____

_____

_____

Date:_____

Wisdom

The fear of the LORD is the beginning of wisdom;
A good understanding have all those who do
His commandments. His praise endures forever.

Psalm 111:10 NKJV

Wisdom is built slowly over a lifetime. It is the sum of every right decision and every honorable deed. It requires the willingness to learn from past mistakes and the faith to seek God's will in decisions both great and small. Wisdom results from countless hours spent in heartfelt prayer. It is forged on the anvil of honorable work and polished by the twin virtues of generosity and humility. Wisdom is a priceless thing, and in today's ever-changing world, America needs it desperately.

Today, let us pray for our leaders, that they might possess the insight and the judgment to direct our nation during this time of adversity and change. And, may God grant us, this generation of American citizens, the collective wisdom to select our leaders wisely and the courage to protect our freedoms vigorously.

Knowledge is horizontal. Wisdom is vertical;
it comes down from above.

Billy Graham

A Prayer

Lord, make me a person of wisdom and
discernment. Lead me in Your ways and teach
me from Your Word so that, in time,
my wisdom might glorify Your kingdom
and Your Son.

—*Amen*

My Personal Reflections:_____

_____

_____

_____

_____

Date:_____

Worry

Be anxious for nothing, but in everything by prayer
and supplication, with thanksgiving, let your requests
be made known to God.

Philippians 4:6 NKJV

If you risk life and limb in service of our country—or if your loved one has chosen to serve and protect America—it is inevitable: You worry. From time to time, you worry about safety, health, finances, family, and countless other concerns, some great and some small.

What should you do when the uncertainties of tomorrow trouble your soul and drain your strength? Take your troubles to God. Take your fears to Him; take your doubts to Him; take your weaknesses to Him; take your sorrows to Him . . . and leave them all there. Seek protection from the One who offers you eternal salvation; build your spiritual house upon the Rock that cannot be moved.

Worry and anxiety are sand in the machinery of life; faith is the oil.

E. Stanley Jones

A Prayer

Lord, You understand my worries and my fears, and You forgive me when I am weak. When my faith begins to waver, help me to trust You more. Then, with Your Holy Word on my lips and with the love of Your Son in my heart, let me live courageously, faithfully, prayerfully, and thankfully today and every day.

—Amen

My Personal Reflections:_____
_____
_____
_____
_____

Date:_____

Worship

I was glad when they said unto me,
Let us go into the house of the LORD.

Psalm 122:1 KJV

All of mankind is engaged in worship . . . of one kind or another. The question is not *if* we worship, but *what* we worship. Some of us choose to worship God. The result is a plentiful harvest of joy, peace, and abundance. Others distance themselves from God by foolishly worshiping things of this earth such as fame, fortune, or personal gratification. To do so is a terrible mistake with eternal consequences.

When we worship God, either alone or in the company of fellow believers, we are blessed. When we fail to worship God, for whatever reason, we forfeit the spiritual riches that are rightfully ours. Every day provides opportunities to put God where He belongs: at the center of our lives. Let us worship Him and only Him, today and always.

Each time, before you intercede, be quiet first and worship
God in His glory. Think of what He can do and how
He delights to hear the prayers of His redeemed people.
Think of your place and privilege in Christ,
and expect great things!

Andrew Murray

A Prayer

When I worship You, Lord, You direct my
path and You cleanse my heart. Let today and
every day be a time of worship and praise.
Let me worship You in everything that I think
and do. Thank You, Lord, for the priceless gift
of Your Son Jesus. Let me be worthy of
that gift, and let me give You the praise
and the glory forever.

—*Amen*

My Personal Reflections:_____

_____

_____

_____

Date:_____

The 1st Psalm

Blessed is the man that walketh not in the counsel of the ungodly, nor standeth in the way of sinners, nor sitteth in the seat of the scornful. But his delight is in the law of the LORD; and in his law doth he meditate day and night. And he shall be like a tree planted by the rivers of water, that bringeth forth his fruit in his season; his leaf also shall not wither; and whatsoever he doeth shall prosper. The ungodly are not so: but are like the chaff which the wind driveth away. Therefore the ungodly shall not stand in the judgment, nor sinners in the congregation of the righteous. For the LORD knoweth the way of the righteous: but the way of the ungodly shall perish.

King James Version

The 23rd Psalm

The LORD is my shepherd; I shall not want. He maketh me to lie down in green pastures: he leadeth me beside the still waters. He restoreth my soul: he leadeth me in the paths of righteousness for his name's sake. Yea, though I walk through the valley of the shadow of death, I will fear no evil: for thou art with me; thy rod and thy staff they comfort me. Thou preparest a table before me in the presence of mine enemies: thou anointest my head with oil; my cup runneth over. Surely goodness and mercy shall follow me all the days of my life: and I will dwell in the house of the LORD for ever.

King James Version

Jesus Teaches About — Worry

Therefore I say to you, do not worry about your life, what you will eat or what you will drink; nor about your body, what you will put on. Is not life more than food and the body more than clothing? Look at the birds of the air, for they neither sow nor reap nor gather into barns; yet your heavenly Father feeds them. Are you not of more value than they? Which of you by worrying can add one cubit to his stature? So why do you worry about clothing? Consider the lilies of the field, how they grow: they neither toil nor spin; and yet I say to you that even Solomon in all his glory was not arrayed like one of these. Now if God so clothes the grass of the field, which today is, and tomorrow is thrown into the oven, will He not much more clothe you, O you of little faith? Therefore do not worry, saying, 'What shall we eat?' or 'What shall we drink?' or 'What shall we wear?' For after all these things the Gentiles seek. For your heavenly Father knows that you need all these things. But seek first the kingdom of God and His righteousness, and all these things shall be added to you. Therefore do not worry about tomorrow, for tomorrow will worry about its own things.

Matthew 6:25-34 NKJV

The Greatest ——— of These is Love

Though I speak with the tongues of men and of angels, but have not love, I have become sounding brass or a clanging cymbal. And though I have the gift of prophecy, and understand all mysteries and all knowledge, and though I have all faith, so that I could remove mountains, but have not love, I am nothing. And though I bestow all my goods to feed the poor, and though I give my body to be burned, but have not love, it profits me nothing. Love suffers long and is kind; love does not envy; love does not parade itself, is not puffed up; does not behave rudely, does not seek its own, is not provoked, thinks no evil; does not rejoice in iniquity, but rejoices in the truth; bears all things, believes all things, hopes all things, endures all things. Love never fails. But whether there are prophecies, they will fail; whether there are tongues, they will cease; whether there is knowledge, it will vanish away. For we know in part and we prophesy in part. But when that which is perfect has come, then that which is in part will be done away. When I was a child, I spoke as a child, I understood as a child, I thought as a child; but when I became a man, I put away childish things. For now we see in a mirror, dimly, but then face to face. Now I know in part, but then I shall know just as I also am known. And now abide faith, hope, love, these three; but the greatest of these is love.

1 Corinthians 13:1-13 NKJV

The Lord's Prayer——

Our Father which art in heaven, Hallowed be thy name. Thy kingdom come. Thy will be done in earth, as it is in heaven. Give us this day our daily bread. And forgive us our debts, as we forgive our debtors. And lead us not into temptation, but deliver us from evil: For thine is the kingdom, and the power, and the glory, for ever. Amen

Matthew 6:9-13 KJV